Reflections In Poetry

"Cowboy And Then Some"

By George C. Burns

ISBN 978-0-615-99168-9

Published by Manzano Publishing and Recording

First Edition

MANZANO: Spanish for Apple Tree

DEDICATION

To my loving Wife and Mother of my four children, who for sixty-five years has been Homemaker, Housekeeper, Cook, Bookkeeper and Secretary. She has without complaint typed, retyped, and then retyped the retyping, two, three, even four times to add a word or rephrase a thought. Never to ask, "Can't you get it right the first Time?"

Also, this is to my children (four), grandchildren (nine), and my great-grandchildren (fifteen). Not to overlook their spouses I love as my own.

They have lovingly and respectively listened to an old man who would read his poetry, perhaps reading the same poem over and over again to any who were present. Most could probably recite any of the hundred or so, seemingly never to tire or at least if they did, they never let it show or keep them from coming to visit.

Come to think about it, they may have just come to see Grandma or give her a break from listening to me! They love Grandma!

FORWARD

I was the third of nine children born to Burley and Gladys (Brunner) Burns. My Father was born in Indian Territory, which is now Southeastern Oklahoma. As a youth, my Father worked on the Charles Goodnight ranch in Texas. He later made his way to New Mexico, to ranch and to farm. There he met my Mother, a schoolteacher. They married in 1921.

Mother's parents made the run in the Oklahoma Land Rush proving up and staking their homestead. At the turn of the century, they moved their family to take up ranching and farming on land that would receive statehood in 1912 as New Mexico.

As children, we never lacked for love from our Parents or Grandparents. We were taught from infancy Obedience, Manners, Respect for others and how to work. We were expected at all times to exhibit what we had been taught.

We made our own entertainment alongside our Parents and Grandparents. Seven of the nine children learned to play several musical instruments. Our Family entertained neighbors, ranchers, farmers as well as cowboys drifting in from time to time.

The family learned poverty and hardship during the Great Depression. Living through the Drought and Dust Bowl of the Thirties.

I had a wealth of experiences as young boy, and have lived a great many more throughout my 86 years. I also have tucked away many stories shared with me by friends and family alike. It is my hope you will enjoy this collection of verses as much as I have enjoyed sharing it with you.

Sincerely,
George C. Burns

Contents

Contents

NEW MEXICO MANZANOS

New Mexico Manzanos beckons me
Return to the old home place once more to see
That call I've heeded time and time again
But that little ranch is not the same as then

Times were hard when we left the old home place
Leaving memories that even time cannot erase
The thirties spread poverty across the land
And changed the way of life we'd come to understand

When Daddy said, "we'd have to pack and go"
And leave the little ranch we loved so
I watched the tears that streamed down Mamma's face
At the thought of leaving Grand-dad's old home place

We didn't know just where we'd go
Then we settled north in Idaho
But Idaho was never home to me
That little ranch I longed once more to see

I hear New Mexico's Manzanos call but then
I know I'll never see
The old home place again
No I'll never see that little ranch again

THE COWBOYS

They don't make cowboys
Like they use to
They never ride a horse
They drive a jeep

They have never slept
Out on the prairie
At night
They sleep on satin sheets

They don't know a doggie
From a bronc
They think that's
A hotdog and a car

They never tip their hat
And tell you "How-Dee"
They're still trying to find
Out who they are

Hats and boots won't ever
Make a cowboy
Neither will a spot
On center stage

There's a few to be found
Though they've grown old
But when you find one
He's like solid gold

THE STAMPEDE

We reached the Pecos at sunset
We were trailing a Chisum herd
Next morning at Horse Head crossing
From the trail boss we waited the word

Head-em up, move-um out was the call at last
It was what we were waiting to hear
While we were all eager to get started
In our hearts it stirred up new fears

We expected there'd be trouble with Indians
We knew that's what others had found
And if there were no raids by Indians
There were rustlers from around Lincoln Town

We headed out toward Fort Stanton
With heavy clouds as the thunder rolled
As lightning split the western sky
Soon death would take its toll

The lead steers all were uneasy
So we called out an extra guard
The roll of thunder and a lightning flash
And the herd was running hard

We were running hard to turn the herd
When they finely settled down
Two of our top hands were missing
Jack and Curley we laid in the ground

DADDY'S SHOES

When we'd walk along the road
Mattered not how hard I tried
I had to run while Daddy walked
To keep close by his side

One day Daddy gave me a horse
And taught me how to ride
Then when we'd walk along the road
We were always side-by-side

But through the years as I grew up
Things changed as all things must
If the hands of time I could turn back
I'd gladly run to keep up

If only I could take his hand in mine
This one thing I'd gladly choose
I'd not just run to keep by his side
I'd much rather fill his shoes

B BAR B RANCH

He reigned up his horse to rest a spell
In the shade of a big oak tree
Looking out across the valley
At the wild horses running free

White-faced cattle cover the land
As far as the eye can see
All of this is the Ranch he owns
It is known as the B Bar B

Fifty years ago he brought his bride to this land
Determined to gain fortune and fame
Now he has wealth beyond compare
Far and wide all know well his name

He toiled and sweat through summer heat
Worked and struggled through winter cold
Still he kept that one thought in mind
It's different now that he's grown old

His wife and family left years ago
He was too busy making money to care
Now when he comes home from riding the range
How he wishes they were waiting there

If only he could turn back the hands of time
All this he'd gladly give
He'd not seek fame and fortune
This time he'd take time to live

A COWBOY'S LIFE

Out in the chuck wagon on the ranch
That they called the lone cottonweed
I'll tell you t'was a lifetime experience to eat
What only old Cookie thought was good

There sat simmering in a pot
What Cookie called rabbit stew
One taste of that awful concoction
All the hands knew t'was witches brew

On the sideboard sat the sour dough
From the biscuits we just had
One smell of that awful sour mixture
You just knew why the biscuits were bad

And there was what Cookie called coffee
Gurgling in an old pot
Like it you didn't have to
But drink it like it or not

But then there's no need complaining
And if you don't like it at all
Then you can just keep right on working
And don't come next time Cookie calls

A DYING BREED

He is just an old fashion cowboy
Not one of the modern drugstore kind
He can rope and tie and brand a steer
Or ride any bronc you can find

He'll work all week at building a fence
Next week he'll be putting up hay
Then round up strays out of the brush
All in the month for his pay

He's just one of a dying breed
He's strong he's gentle he's kind
He don't have to tell you how good he is
If you can't see this in him you're blind

He has a love for the open range
And to sleep under a star filled sky
He knows he has the best way of life
A way that money can't buy

WILD HORSES

Wild horses on the mesa
Eagle in a cloudless sky
Dust devils in the valley
Where the water holes gone dry

The grass is gone from the mesa
With the winter coming on
Rains didn't come this summer
The grass in the valleys gone

Wild horses on the mesa
Thirst under a scorching sun
Search for grass and water
Slowly dying one by one

Eating bark and brush on the mesa
Soon the winter wind will blow
What grass is left in the valley
Will lie buried under snow

While the ranchers in the valley
Watch their plight in vain
They've sold off all their cattle
Cause the rains just never came

And over above the rim rock
The vultures circle high
As another wild horse stumbles
Another wild horse dies

Old stallion running with his herd
Proud heads once held high
Now walk with slow and measured step
As one by one they die

BILLIE SANCHEZ

I remember Billie Sanchez
When I was just a kid
I tried to be like Billie
In everything he did

The way he sat the saddle
The way he'd whirl a rope
Some day I'd be just like Billie
Even in the way he'd talk

I'd listen to all his stories
And I'd hang on to every word
He taught me how to tame a bronc
And how to move a herd

Some said, "He came from Texas
Where he worked for the Goodnight brand"
He said, "He learned to ride a horse
By the time he'd learned to stand"

Billie was the best all around cowboy
In New Mexico's Fairland
In fact I'm sure he was the best
Either side of the Rio Grand

A RANCH IN THE VALLEY

Hidden deep in a valley where I long to go
There's a ranch on the Pecos in New Mexico
That's where I was born and lived as a boy
A Little Mexican pony was my pride and joy

I grew up reckless and I grew up wild
With Mother and Daddy I was their only child
Dear Mother and Daddy sit home all alone
Wondering if their wayward boy will come home

They think I must be dead
And that's just as well
Because for ninety nine years
I'll be locked in this cell

I'd just turned sixteen when I first left home
A rounding up cattle then I started to roam
I started drinking and gambling to fit in with the crowd
Of the life that I've lived I'm not very proud

A robbery was planned it was just for the thrill
Not intending to shoot not planning to kill
But three men lay dead as we rode away
The Judge said, "Your guilty now boys you must pay."

So come all you young fellows and heed my advice
When choosing your friends you better think twice
Or you just like me for your wrongs you will pay
And in some lonesome prison you'll be locked away

CHARLIE

The young man's name was Charlie
He said, "Jones was his family name."
Charlie came to our ranch in New Mexico
From somewhere on the Texas plains

He said, "He would do most anything,
And he'd gladly work for his keep."
He said, "He'd been on the road three days
Without as much as a bite to eat."

As Charlie stood there talking
Desperation on his face
Dad turned and said to Mother
"Set old Charlie a place."

Then after we finished eating
Dad and Charlie walked outside
I overheard old Charlie say
He was looking for horses to ride

He looked over the wild bunch in the corral
Flipping a loop on the best one with pride
He fashioned a surcingle with a piece of rope
I'll tell you old Charlie could ride

As that horse left the ground
He bucked twisted and turned
He tested old Charlie for all he had learned
Although he was barely fifteen years old

It was here Charlie's reputation began to unfold
As he waved his hat with a grin and a yell
His way with a horse old Charlie knew well
His skill with a horse I'll make no bones
There was never another like Charlie Jones

COTTONWOOD JUSTICE

They said, he grew up a loner
He never listened to his Ma
Just a no good shiftless drifter
Who never knew his Pa

It was in the town of Magdalena
At the height of the mining boom
That by the Marshall he was told
In this town for you there's no room

He drifted in and out of Lincoln City
For a time he run with Billie the kid
Until the law caught up with Billie
And he paid for the crimes that he did

For awhile he was seen around White Oaks
Then as a drover for the Chisholm brand
It was a long rope and a running iron
That finally tipped his hand

On the spot he met Cottonwood Justice
A short drop to the end of a rope
To out run a New Mexico Posse
Was a rustlers only hope

HARD TIMES

Mama and Daddy never took a vacation
It was all they could do to keep the family fed
They were up each morning before sun-up
It was past midnight before they went to bed

In the bean fields Mama worked alongside Daddy
She could do the work of any man
This I learned quite young from Mama and Daddy
You can do more than you think you can

Daddy made shoes for all the family
With leather from hides that he had tanned
While Mama made soap to do the laundry
Then washed it on a rub board by hand

From flour sacks she made hers and sister's dresses
By a coal oil light she altered hand me downs
The eggs the chicken laid and the butter that she made
She'd trade for groceries when she'd go to town

Mama did the cooking on a wood stove
Daddy hauled the wood out of the hills
Daddy said, "Hard work would keep us healthy"
And Mama wasn't one for pushing pills

In the evenings we would gather around the organ
And sing the songs that Mama and Daddy knew
What I'd give if only I could go back
And harmonize the way that we used to

DESPAIR

He gently takes her hand in his
Tenderly kissed her on the brow
Said, "We'll make it through all this yet
But as of now I know not how."

We've been through all of this before
It's same both day and night
You know we've heard it said many times
"At the end of the tunnel there's a light."

We've waited now seem since time began
Oh! Good! At last, I think we'll win.
Ah the comfort and solitude of home we seek
Grocery shopping done for another week!

Illustration by Grandson
Christopher C. Burns

J.L. MERRITT

Old Jerry's a genuine cowboy
Forty dollars a month and his keep
Brushing cattle out of the hills
Riding a horse not a jeep

Some might think him a small man
Seventy-two inches less three
But in Jerry's chest beats a heart of pure gold
He's a big man among men to me

Just a rodeo bareback bronc rider
When he forks the old bronc in the chute
For an eight-second ride the gates opens wide
And he comes out raking the brute

Man what a ride Jerry's glued to his hide
As the crowd all wait for the horn
Jerry loses his seat tries to land on his feet
Eats enough dirt to make a small farm

Oh what a sight Jerry's name up in lights
That's where we all know it belongs
In the Hall of fame you'll see Jerry's name
Along with his guitar and songs

You'll see Jerry Merritt's name up high
In the Rockabilly hall of fame
For what he has done
With his guitar and songs

LAKOTA

Proud he stands upon a hill
Looking out upon the land
Once covered with the mighty Buffalo
Where his brothers in battle made a stand

He recalls the stories his elders tell
The treachery of the Whitman they knew
Woman children and the old were killed
Treaties broken were not just a few

Dead or dying his brothers lay
None their lives sought to save
They fell before the blue coats guns
They'd not be the Whiteman's slave

The westward push of the wagon trains
Drove the Redman from off their land
To starve on the reservations
Or to be slaughtered if he made a stand

Until the battle of the little big horn
When the Redman made his suffering felt
In the battle with hated yellow hair and his troops
A divisive blow was dealt

NEW MEXICO DIRT FARMER

The old man rocked back on a rickety old chair
Running his fingers through graying hair
He gazed out through the dust at a sun-parched land
And the crops that he'd planted now covered with sand

Cause it hadn't rained since way back when
And so next year he'd try again
But he'd been through all this before
And all he could remember was being poor

He'd have to sell the livestock and mortgage the farm
To buy more seed and food and keep the family warm
Then one more year he'd plant and toil
Another crop failure he'd move off the soil

And if he had to move away
He vowed to return again someday
Even though he couldn't see just how
If to the whim of nature he had to bow

**In memory of the farmers in the pinto bean capitol
Of the world Mountainair, New Mexico
And the dust bowl of the 1930's**

MY FRIEND BILLIE

Old Billie was a friend of mine
I could talk to him any time
About the things I felt inside
From him my feeling I didn't have to hide

He always had a hearing ear
I would ride over hill and dale
Pretending to be
On a cattle trail

I got old Billie when I was five
A finer horse was never alive
At least that's the way it seemed to me
When on his back I was so carefree

Then Dad sold old Billie one spring day
And from New Mexico we moved away
Those times I still recall and then
If I could I'd live them all again

NO QUITTER

On the top rail of the old corral
A young bronc peeler sat
With his hand to his jaw he could feel it swell
With a roguish tilt of his hat

He softly spoke to the old outlaw paint
Old feller I ain't done with you yet
You've only throwed me fifteen times
Now I see you're starting to sweat

Oh I've been throwed harder and higher
Here I am eating dirt once again
But when I hit the saddle the next time
Here's a promise old boy you'll not win

I'll have you know I'm no quitter
You may think you've wounded my pride
But when I get all that ornery peeled off
I know there's a good cow horse inside

So I'll give you a ten minute breather
While I get a steak on this eye
And when I come back old feller
We'll give it another try

THE 30's

In my mind the memories flow
To our home in Mountainair New Mexico
Three miles east down the railroad track
Home to me just a three room shack

Times were hard and the people poor
The wolf was always at the door
The shake of a hand was good as gold
Respect was taught to the young for the old

The great depression effected everyone
Some days the dust would hide the sun
In times of need a friend was there
With those less fortunate they were willing to share

Honor was treasured and never sold
A way of life for both young and old
Now it's only in memory I go back
To Mountainair and that three room shack

THE BLACK STALLION

He's a hard working bronc riding cowboy
He's in the saddle before sun-up each day
Out riding the range or building a fence
At times he'll be putting up hay

A black stallion runs with a wild bunch
He's claimed that old boy for himself
There's work around the ranch that needs to be done
He'll just have to put it on the shelf

The roof on the barn needs some shingles
The bronc corral needs some repairs
There's a song in his heart a smile on his face
You'll never see him putting on airs

He's in love with the rancher's pretty daughter
He'll ask for her hand in the spring
And from his rodeo winnings
He'll buy her a big diamond ring

His spare time he spends out on the Mesa
He's building a wild horse corral
That fiery black stallion that runs with the herd
That Wiley old boy he knows well

He'll bring the broncs down from the Mesa
And break them so they can be sold
The fiery black stallion he'll keep for himself
He's worth far more to him than the gold

Continued on page 38

Marilyn Dagustad
2009

He'll train him for cutting and roping
Doggin hazen and such
He'll learn all the things a good cow-horse should know
Start stop turn and wheel at a touch

He's in love with the rancher's pretty daughter
He'll ask for her hand in the spring
And from his rodeo winnings
He'll buy her a big diamond ring

Then he'll follow the rodeo circuit
When the branding is done in the spring
He'll lease the black stallion
To any of the boys and a share of the winnings he'll
gain

He's a hard working bronc riding cowboy
In the saddle fore sun-up each day
Riding the range or building a fence
At times he'll be putting up hay

The roof on the barn needs some shingles
The bronc corral needs some repairs
There's a song in his heart a smile on his face
You'll never see him putting on airs

He's in love with the rancher's pretty daughter
He'll ask for her hand in the spring
And from his rodeo winnings
He'll buy her that big diamond ring

THE FALLING LEAVES

The young girls sit around the old ones
They learn to sew the buckskin dress
While the young boys play at hunting
Each trying to be the best

The women make clothes from the hides
Of the deer and the buffalo
To protect their families from the cold
And the winter winds that blow

The green grass in the summer camp
Has turned to a golden brown
And leaves on the trees on the hillside
Are slowly falling to the ground

The summer days have come and gone
And fall comes to an end
It's time to take the teepees down
And move to the rivers bend

There's meat from the summer hunts
Dried by the sun and wind
There'll be food for all in camp to eat
Until winter comes to an end

THE BULL RIDER

The old bull stood
And just looked around
The next bull rider
He'd stomp into the ground

A young bull rider heaved a sigh
Shook his head gloves slapping his thigh
His eyes open wide mouth even wider
This is the bull and he the next rider

He looked at the bull
Amazed at his size
He must be three feet between the eyes
He couldn't help but show surprise

That old bull the ornery cuss
Was about the size of a greyhound bus
He had one horn sawed off
The other one broken

Now he knew why the boys all were joking
An uglier bull he'd never seen
With that much ugly
He had to be mean

THE RACE

In the starting gate on the race track
The old stallion took his place
Where he had faced many challenges
And always finished in first place

The youngster in the gate beside him
Would show all just what he had
Beyond a shadow of a doubt
He'd now show up old Dad

The starting gate swung open
Each bolted from their place
The old stallion coming from behind
Dirt squarely in his face

Down the track with hoofs a flying
The two now side by side
In the turn the young colt falters
As the old stallion now gains stride

Now it's down the home stretch
The finish line the end of the race
The young colt comes in number four
The old stallion still the Ace

The moral of this story
If you will please listen well
It's not the starting gate or the racetrack
But the finish line that tells

REMINISCING

Often when we reminisce
A fond embrace a tender kiss
A fleeting glimpse of yester years
At times the memories bring a tear

But mostly we recall the joy
Of raising a family two girls two boys
Each holds a very special place
As their lives we endeavor to retrace

While others may have caused their parents pain
Parental approval ours sought to gain
To run with the crowd was not their thought
But obediently followed what they'd been taught

As we watch Grandchildren Great-Grand children too
And see such training carried through
Looking back on the trials and fears
It's all been worth it these sixty-five years

TRAIL OF TEARS

He walks along the river
That's the name he's called
Eyes now dry from tears he's cried
Still the memories he recalls

Hearts and spirits broken
All down through the years
The greed of man for gold and land
The long walk the trail of tears

There are some who don't believe him
Some say he's lost his mind
Even though he's lost his sight
To injustice he's not blind

Great Chieftains men of honor
Cheated lied to and deceived
By the white man's written treaties
And spoken words that they believed

The massacre at Sand Creek
The one at Wounded Knee
Crushed and driven from their land
No more to wonder free

He walks along the river
In the twilight of his years
His heart is filled with sadness
His eyes with unshed tears

TRUE TO THE BADGE

He rode into town at sunset
Covered with dust from the trail
Swinging lightly from the saddle
Tied his horse at the hitching rail

He pushed open the door walked to the bar
As he turned to face the door
You could see the gun slung low on his hip
Tied down a big forty four

He had a snarl on his lip and a firm set jaw
And death in his stony gray eyes
That said the first man to cross him
Would be the next man to die

It was plain to see he was on the run
From the hollow look in his eyes
He seemed to be about fifteen years old
From the crack in his voice and his size

Continued on page 48

The Marshal knew of his dastardly deeds
He vowed he'd make an arrest
The kid seemed not at all worried
With his gun he'd laid many to rest

He bragged the law would never take him
That he was the fastest gun around
And if he faced the Marshal in the street
The Marshal would lay dead on the ground

They faced each other next day at noon
Two shots rang out with one sound
The Marshal took off his badge and his gun
And dropped them by the kid on the ground

They didn't hear his breaking heart
They couldn't see the unshed tears
Or know the kid was his brother's son
He hadn't seen in ten years

FORESIGHT

Foresight is like signposts
On the road of life
Which if heeded most often
We avoid trouble and strife

Hindsight too can help us see
Where in the future we ought to be
Not just the things in the road behind
But a sense of direction in the future find

At times those we love
We may misuse
We beg they'll forgive
Not just excuse

FACE PROBLEMS OF LIFE HEAD ON

My old daddy told me when I was very young
When problems that you face in life
Knock you to the ground
And when your praises go unsung
Just pick yourself up
Dust yourself off
Don't just lay there on the ground
Standing on both your feet
You can wage a better fight

A HEARING EAR

Is there something I don't know
That you should tell me son
That's weighing heavy on your mind
Something you may have done

You know I'll help you see it through
Remembering that you're just a youth
And if others were involved with you
Don't be afraid to speak the truth

In your life we want you to be a success
And be proud of the things you've done
So the guidelines were established
Are meant to protect not stifle your fun

So remember son your Mother and I
Once were young like you
We understand the way you feel
And we'll always be there for you

So anytime you want to talk
About the things you are uncertain
Know I'll give a hearing ear
And relieve your conscience that's hurting

'JUNIE MAE'

Ya orta dance with the one what brung ya
Or yur gonna be a walkin home
I ain't a flirtin with other gals
So leave them other fellers alone

An dance wuth the one what brung ya
Or ya don't get brung again
So if yur hankern to start a walkin
Yur pa said to be home by ten

So Junie Mae if I be yur feller
Wul ya better start a lettin it show
Eer I'll be callin this courtin off
An I'll be fer lettin ya go

Ya orta dance wuth the one who brung ya
An I ain't a tellin ya twice
The heart strings yur bustin tonight
Tis gonna be mighty hard to splice

So dance wuth the one what brung ya
Or yur sure to be a walkin home
Now I ain't a flirtin wuth no other gal
Just leave them fellers alone

George C. Burns Age 4

Illustration by Great-Grandson:
Hayden Curtis Burns (8 years old)
Artist in training for my next book!

GRAND DAD

Down a country road across the railroad track
Without a thought of looking back
I was leaving home 'cause I was mad
And no one cared except Granddad

In his blacksmith shop standing by the forge
All called us big and little George
On his face a big broad grin
I see you're running away from home again

A half a mile is a long way for a Young man to walk
Here turn this forge blower then we'll talk
Life's responsibilities one cannot shirk
So if you're leaving home you'll have to work

Oh yes I know you're real strong
You'd not do anything you thought wrong
And you'll face the trials in life real bold
But who'll give a job to a four year old?

GRANDAD'S OLD HAT

I vowed I'd say a million times
Fixed it firmly in my mind
That I'd wear no more hand me downs
Though I knew it was meant to be kind

One day while feeling so alone
In the porch swing where I sat
Much to the joy and my surprise
On my head Granddad set his old hat

Mind you this was not a hand me down
This was my greatest prize
Mattered not that others found
The old hat was not my size

With Granddad's old hat upon my head
I felt about ten feet tall
I didn't care what others said
To me it didn't matter at all

"PATCHES"

He angrily clinched his little fists
And defiantly stood his ground
He'd take them all on one at a time
When the others were not around

He'd been the brunt of their taunting jeers
He looked his tormenters in the eye
He would never bow his head in shame
Or let them see him cry

His Mother said, "patches were honorable
He should be thankful for hand me downs"
Mattered not if the shirtsleeves were too short
And the pants were too big around

And remember they are just bullies
When they jerk your hat off and run
Just pay them no attention
And they won't think it so much fun

He tried his best to ignore them
And heed what his Mother said
But if they called him patches one more time
He swore he'd bust some heads

REACH FOR THE STARS

Goals in life quite often change
From the better to the worse
And yet to have no goal at all
Is even a greater curse.

So set your goals real high my son
And in doing so reach for the stars
Remember you're never a failure
If you always know who you are

Don't' pretend to be of noble birth
There's no wrong side of the track
Remember the things you say and do in life
Have a way of coming back

Never forget the way that you were raised
By Father and Mother who care
Even if at times you do forget
Remember they are always there

MEMORIES

The lonesome whistle of a midnight train
A country road and a summer rain
The soft white blanket of winter's first snow
And the gentle caress of moonlight glow

Flashing lightning in a stormy sky
Signals all that rain is nearby
The rolling thunder and storm winds blow
Summer's sunset after glow

Childhood's memories of New Mexico
Jack rabbits and the cottontails
The prairie dog barks the coyote wails
Whippoorwill and the meadowlark

Their love song sings from morn to dark
The curlew and mourning dove
Also sing their songs of love
These I remember from long ago
As a boy in Mountainair New Mexico

Miss Dennis' first grade class 1932
Front row 2nd from the right
George C. Burns

MOUNTAINAIR NEW MEXICO

In a little school where I used to go
Where teachers taught what we should know
How to read how to write to do
Arithmetic and get the answers right

A few I still recall their names
This their only call to fame
That those they started on their way
Years later think fondly on their names

There was Miss Dennis who taught me how to dream
Miss Arnold taught me self-esteem
Mrs. Williams run a disciplinary ship
Mr. Phillips too would take no lip

Mr. A.R. Wood levied praise
Lauded parents for how I was raised
When a purse I found to him was turned
The loss soon after by the owner learned

The names of others I no longer know
This was school in Mountainair New Mexico

THE LOYAL RESIST A LIE

Loyalty is not just a spoken word
Uttered only to be heard
Loyalty is a noble deed
Where hatred and mistrust never feed

So when life's road takes a sudden turn
Remember the things that you have learned
Embrace the one's both tried and true
The ones who have sacrificed for you

Permit no one to
Besmirch their name
If you do it's you
That must bear the shame

BUDDY DOGETT

Down at the river bank one day
I watched the river flow on its way
And as the river boiled and churned
To my boyhood days my thoughts returned

As a friend of mine along with some others
A one armed boy one more and two brothers
Sailing the river without a care
When one of the boys to take a dare

Climbed the mast not counting the cost
Into the river the boys were tossed
One of the brothers couldn't swim
So Buddy to safety assisted him

Turned to help another so he wouldn't drown
But before reaching him Buddy went down
A week went by before he was discovered
Three miles downriver the body recovered

I often think of this young man brave
When a friend in danger he tried to save
Never once did he count the cost
For the sake of a friend his life he lost

HOLES IN THE WIND

Seems I'm trying to walk on water
And punch holes in the wind
It's hard to tell which way you're going
When you don't know where you've been

To try and tell what's on my mind
And helping you to understand
Is like trying to stop the ocean tide
Or hold the oceans in my hands

I can't still the howling winds
And I can only walk on land
I can't stop the sun from setting
After all I'm just a man

No I can't walk on water
Or punch holes in the wind
I can't tell which way I'm going
When I can't tell where I've been

WISDOM

A dear wise old man once told my son
Every man carries two sacks
One he fills with his faults
And carries it on his back

Then with the faults of others
He fills the other just half that size
And carries that one on his chest
Always before his eyes

So take the sack from off your chest
Carry it on your back
Work hard to correct your own faults
Of them you'll find no lack

And don't worry about faults of others
If with what's right they just don't fit
Just leave the matter in God's hands
And he'll take care of it

SMELL THE ROSES

Take time to smell the roses
As you travel life's highway
Don't put off until tomorrow
What you should have done today

Yesterday is dead and gone
And tomorrow never comes
Today like the fleeting hands of time
It's here then quickly gone

Today is yesterday's tomorrow
And tomorrow's yesterday
So smell the roses while you can
While today is still today

SUMMER LOVE

They met one Sunday afternoon
Both were in their teens
She wore a pretty Gingham dress
He wore old blue jeans

They dated through the summer
Then he gave her a ring
Then he went away to school
They vowed to marry in the spring

She promised she would wait for him
He promised he'd be true
Although they didn't know it then
This neither one would do

He soon met a girl at school
She met her brother's friend
Not what either one had planned
Their plans came to an end

The two at school went separate ways
He recalled what he left back home
She and her brother's friend broke up
Each wondered why they had roamed

LIVE AND LEARN

At sixteen he knew it all
He could learn no more
He put on his hat and coat
Walked out and slammed the door

Ah he breathed at last I'm free
Now I'm my own boss
But in time he sadly learned
His gain is not worth the loss

He's now in the real world
This is the school of hard knocks
Where he makes all his decisions
That mostly pelts him like rocks

Oh how he'd like to undo the hurt
If only his shame he could hide
He'd like to admit to all he was wrong
But he can't put aside his pride

He's now come to understand
But why did it take so long
He's now telling his sixteen year old
Who thinks his Dad is wrong

EARLY SETTLERS

They carved out of the wilderness
A place to call home
They would settle here
No more to roam

Land and water enough to go around
No better place could they have found
They faced the threat of Indian raids
Hardships severe and still they stayed

These were principled men
They were not just fools
They earned respect
They established schools

They raised their families
They tamed the land
For a neighbor in need
They'd lend a hand

Their supplies were hauled from Watertown
By oxen teams the only source around
Rain didn't fall and the dust would blow
Crops withered and died only tumbleweeds would grow

Children wondered women would wring their hands
Still these men stayed and tilled the land
All looked and prayed for a better day
With broken spirit some moved away

Through it all
Some persevered
Stayed on the land
They held so dear

EMPTY ROCKING CHAIR

The old rocking chair sets empty
Where he would sit and chat
And the peg at the side of the kitchen door
Where he would hang his old hat.

His old fiddle sets on the piano
When once cradled in his hands
He'd tap his foot and draw the bow
The music he made was grand

The old piano sets against the wall
Keys once caressed by her hands
The music they made for the country dance
I'll tell you beat all the big bands

It's been many years, but I still recall
Sweet music how it filled the air
Hank and Hazel and the Plano Grange hall
In memory I often go there

In memory of my Father and Mother-law
Hank and Hazel Everson
By George C. Burns 1-20-2009

My wonderful wife
Priscilla Jean (Everson) Burns

BLACK COFFEE

I recall the day I met the girl
Working in an Ice cream store
I said, "I think I'll have a coffee,"
As I walked in through the door

She stirred in cream and sugar
When she brought my coffee back
I couldn't bring myself to say
I drink my coffee black

I watched her work the counter
Serving each and every one
While she kept my coffee coming hot
Until I said, "I'm done."

Such beauty, grace in motion
In my life I'd never seen
I knew someday that she would be
My wife and lovely queen.

So I paid the check and left a tip
She said, "Thanks do hurry back."
And as I walked out through the door
I felt her eyes upon my back

She sure made good coffee
So I kept going back
I finely had to tell the girl
I drink my coffee black

That was more than sixty-five years ago
My mind keeps going back
To the day I met my darling wife
And I still drink my coffee black

COME WALK WITH ME

Come walk with me dear Katie
Just take my outstretched hand
And as we walk together
I hope you'll understand

Come walk with me dear Katie
Tell me you'll share my life
And I'll pledge all my love for you
If you'll please be my wife

Come walk with me dear Katie
My love will ne'er grow cold
We'll share our love for each other
A love as pure as gold

I'll walk with you dear Marvin
Yes I'll give you my hand
Neither one of us need say a word
For we both understand

I'll walk with you dear Marvin
I'll share with you my life
And as I pledge my love for you
I'll gladly be your wife

Please take my hand dear Katie
We've laughed and shed some tears
And the love and joy we've shared together
Throughout these seventy years

I'll hold your hand dear Marvin
Just as in the days of old
The love we've shared so true and real
And genuine as pure gold

We still hold each other's hand
Our love pledge to each other
Looking back these seventy years
We'd still choose one another

FIFTY YEARS

If I my life I could live over
The things I've said and done
One thing I can say for certain
For wife I'd still choose the same one

My wife to would have a choice though
I might not be the one
Cause fifty years of marriage
I know I've been more pain than fun

I WONDER

I wonder if you miss me
Or if you even you care
And do you cry yourself to sleep
At night when I'm not there

Have you found another
To love and take my place
When he holds you close to kiss you
Do you sometimes see my face

I didn't know that you were leaving
Until you'd gone away
Darling please forgive me
For those words I didn't say

Don't you know that I still love you
As on the day we wed
And I could never say of you
The things you thought I said

I know you think that I was wrong
Now we both must pay
You're always in my heart and mind
Every night and day

LOVE UNDERSTANDS

Love is blind so some will say
But I see love another way
True love when another does select
Will search for good not defect
And so you why not be kind
Then you will see with an open mind
And understand that love's not blind

MY WIFE MY LIFE

You were just a girl when first we met
I loved you from the start
But the hand that you'd been dealt
Crushed the love out of your heart

I vowed I'd win your heart and hand
And take you for my bride
When we walked along the street
My heart welled up with pride

It was in the fall we said our vows
To love honor and obey
I loved you then with all my heart
Though I love you more today

You are still my girl my only world
You'll still be until the day I die
The things that life has put you through
In my heart for you I cry

REFLECTIONS AT 85

Is the old ranch house still standing
Where I spent many boyhood days?
With the love of my Grandparents
Before time called them away

Does the windmill still pump water
As it did so long ago?
When I was just a suntanned kid
On the ranch in New Mexico

Are the stock tanks filled with water
Or has the well run dry?
Are the cattle fat and lazy
Do eagles circle in the sky?

Do the prairie dogs and rattle snakes
Claim the old ranch as their own?
Or do the rabbits and the coyotes
Make the little ranch their home?

Do the trains still blow their whistle
As they roll on down the line?
And do the nuts still taste the same
Gathered from the Pinion pine?

Does the northeast wind in winter
Still bring the snow and cold?
And do the dust clouds fill the sky
As they did so long ago?

Do they still haul wood from the Manzanos
To stoke the kitchen fires?
Do granddads still love grandsons
And from the questions never tire?

Do the gates swing on the hinges
Granddad fashioned at his forge?
And does the smells from grandmas kitchen
Still linger in and out of doors?

Do little children still run and play
Without a fear or care?
Is there any place on Earth
Like that little ranch in Mountainair?

DON'T ASK ME TO DANCE

At times I've heard my children say
Pa why don't you ever dance with Ma?
Now my Grandchildren ask the same question
Beats all I ever saw

To do fancy steps on a dance hall floor
I've never been so inclined
But I did learn to dance in the woodshed
With a belt across my behind

I learned the two-step and the jitterbug
And new steps there was no lack
My Dad was a talented drummer
His drum was quite often my back

Now if you learned to dance like I did
In the woodshed not a dance floor
To the music of a razor strap
You wouldn't be hankering for more

MY WIFE AND FAMILY

You can never understand
How much you mean to me
I could never do you wrong
I've never wanted to be free

I gave you my heart and hand
When I gave you my name
More than sixty-five years ago
And I still feel the same

I never had great wealth or fame
All I had to give
Was a good name to wear with honor
And the truth I've tried to live

You gave me a family
Two darling girls two wonderful boys
Each one dearer than life to me
Each one has brought me joy

Each of them has married
And have families and a home
If I may have failed some
That's no reason to fail their own

And at last when I lay down
And close my eyes in rest
I pray that God can say, well done!
And that we've all stood the test

NO RETIREMENT

Don't try to make me retire
Because you say I'm past 65
Let me keep doing the work
I've always done till I'm past 95

Your old rocking chair has no appeal
Just why should I rust out
You can shout from the mountain top
I'd much rather wear out

When at last I'm past 75
If I can still move about
If I can do the work I love
For joy I'll jump and shout

Your old rocking chair has no appeal
Just why I should rust out
You can shout it from the highest mountain
I'd much rather wear out

THE TOUCH OF GOD'S HAND

I've watched the dance of the northern lights
On the stage of a winter night
And a diamond studded black velvet sky
Majestic redwoods towering high

The sky with a sunset after glow
Summer rains and winter snow
Waving fields of golden grain
Emerald green the rolling plains

Snow capped mountains touch the sky
Raging rivers rushing by
Love as true as an arrows flight
All things in life that bring delight

This I've come to understand
Is the loving touch of God's own hand
All of this who could ask for more
And yet there is I've children four

I've known love and laughter
Joy and tears
And the same loving wife
These past sixty-five years

THE EVERSONS

Out of the land of a thousand lakes
These hardy pioneers came
They were immigrants from Norway
Everson was the family name

No safety of a wagon train
This little pioneer band
They carved a place in History
In the untamed Dakota land

They endured the winter blizzards
And the blazing summer sun
They staked their claims and turned the soil
Their homesteads had begun

They faced the threat of Indians
In this wild and untamed land
And if a neighbor was in need
They'd always lend a hand

They raised their families with high morals
Always to God and self be true
A man is no better than his word
Matters not what others say or do

1922 Henry (Hank) D. Everson
Columbia South Dakota

SHUT-OUT

The umpire brushed dirt
From off home plate
As on the mound
The young pitcher waits

Gloved hand on his hip
He'll give his all
From home plate the umpire
Cries batter up! Play ball!

The pitcher winds up
He delivers the ball
The batter swings
Hits air that's all

As each batter stands to
Face the mound
The ball is delivered
Each batter put down

The way it looks
There is no doubt
That for H. D. Everson
Another shut-out

THE BACK SIDE OF HAPPY

Now I'm living on the back side of happy
That's one place I never thought I'd be
But I'm living on the back side of happy
Since the day you walked out on me

Darling you once said you'd always love me
That you'd always be right by my side
Now I'm living on the back side of happy
Cause each of us had too much selfish pride

NOT UNTIL

When the sun and moon
Fall from the sky
And all the rivers run uphill
That's when I'll stop loving you
Darling not until

Never feel that I don't care
That just could never be
I love you now
And always will
Longer than eternity

If the sun the moon and stars above
All could testify
They'd all swear
My love for you
Could never ever die

So when the sun and moon
Fall from the sky
And all the rivers run up hill
That's when I'll stop loving you
But darling not until

SOUTH DAKOTA

Cold the winter wind does blow
High the swirling drifting snow
In the farmhouse safe and warm
Watch outside the winter's first storm
Stock well fed and in the barn
It's winter on the Everson farm

THE LEGACY

When I first met darling wife
All I had to give
Was my name I'd borne with honor
And the truth I'd tried to live

I gave her my heart and hand when I gave her my name
More than sixty-five years ago and I still feel the same

She's given me a family two darling girls two boys
Each one dearer than life to me
Each one has brought me joy
Now each of them have married and have children of
Their own
If I may have failed some I pray they don't fail their
own

If in time when I lie down and close my eyes in death
I pray that God can say
Well done and we've all stood the test

I've neither fame or fortune but this legacy I give
My good name I kept with honor and the truth I've tried
To live

So keep this legacy in wisdom
To your children pass it on
If some fail to live by it it's not the legacy gone wrong

WEDDING RING

It's not just a wedding ring
That keeps her in my life
It takes more than just a wedding ring
Between a husband and a wife

She's my sunshine every morning
She's that dream I dream at night
Just a smile from her sweet lips
Makes everything all right

Like oil on troubled waters
When the raging seas run high
When we face the storms in life
It's her that keeps us dry

She's like a rock foundation
She puts meaning in my life
The Mother of my children
She's my Darling wife

THE SATURDAY NIGHT DANCE

It's just an old fiddle
With one broken string
And to those who might see it
It don't mean a thing
But to me that old fiddle
Fond memories recall
Of the Saturday night dance
At the Plano grange hall

I recall Hank and Hazel
And the songs we would play
At the Saturday night dance
How the couples would sway
A dusty old piano
Sets there on the stage
To tell a sweet story
Of a different age

From most of the keys
The ivories all gone
Still through my mind
Run all those old songs
Hank and Hazel are gone
And we've all moved away
The Plano grange hall
Still stands there unused today

In memory of my Father and Mother-law
Hank and Hazel Everson
By George C. Burns – 1-20-2009

TO MY DAUGHTERS

When first I held you in my arms
And gazed upon your face
I knew this was Daddy's little girl
In my heart none could take your place
An extension of my very being
Another reason for me to live
As I worked away from home each day
I carried that vision close to my heart
I knew my family of which you were one
Meant more to me than life itself

Then came the day
When I saw you in a different light
A grown up beautiful woman
Where did the between years go
Today that beauty goes far beyond that of a physical
kind
True beauty to the depth of your very being
With families of your own
Words can never express
The love and pride I have for you
Although you are a woman in every sense of the word
You'll always be my little girl
I'm so proud of what you have become
And will yet come to be
Know that I love you very much

TO MY SONS

I recall the day that you were born
You were my little boy
An extension of my very being
While I worked away from home each day
My every working hour belonged to my family
Of which you were one

One day while sitting down to dinner
Behold you had become a man
You were all grown-up
Where did the between years go

Suddenly I must let go
As you started families of your own
Today you are a man
In every sense of the word
But you will always be my little boy

Words can never express
The love and pride in my heart for you
And what you have become
And will yet come to be
Know that I love you very much

"PRIDE"

He wonders in and out of life
This uninvited guest
At times demanding center stage
Doing so without request

Although he's known by others
Most of them him deride
He's equally uninvited there
He's known as selfish pride

At times he'll speak for everyone
Before they are aware
Cutting each one to the heart
As if they didn't care

And he'll continue this uninvited guest
Doing damage and leaving doubt
Until each one has had enough
And together throw him out

WHERE

I've looked the whole place over
I've looked both high and low
I used it only yesterday
Pray tell where did it go?
I know it must be somewhere
But Somewhere I just don't know
I know when I finished using it
I put the thing away
Someone must have moved it
Or did it just fly away?

Henry (Hank) D. Everson

YOU CAN NEVER GO BACK

I thought that I'd return and see
Where in years gone by was home to me
To see the fields of waving grain
I know I'll soon be home again

I see my Dad coming from the barn
And Mothers kitchen all sweet and warm
The crack of dawn the rooster crows
The smell of smoke the swirling snow

Just a few of my memories of long ago
To go back I had to once again
To that special place in the river bend
The drive way leads to house and barn

And that grove of trees the Everson farm
Oh no! The Everson School has been torn down
And the barns been moved almost to town
Where the house so proudly stood

There's not a trace not a piece of wood
No matter how the heart may yearn
You can't go back
You just return

HURRY BACK

It's always hard to say good-by
To friends we all love so
And send them off to someplace new
When they would rather stay then go

It's not good-by but just so long
Of our love there is no lack
Matters not how short or long the stay
Your always welcome back

But you'll make new friends of others
You're just that kind of folks
New friends can never replace the old
That's a truism not a joke

So here is to the both of you
Know our love is true and strong
A fond fare-well do hurry back
Don't let the parting be to long

TIMMIE – TIM – TIMOTHY

From Father and Mother, you've had true affection
As they've guided you in the right direction.
Helping you grow in wisdom from above
And to serve Jehovah the God of love.

And as they've watched you grow with pride,
They've prayed from Jehovah you'll not turn aside.
But they've now done the best they can
Helping you grow from boy to a man.

And we've watched you grow from two years of age
Life for you turns another page.
Where life takes you whether near or far
Never forget just who you are.

Though long or short may be your days
To other God's give not your praise.
And to Jehovah God always give your all
Then from his favor you'll never fall.

OUR GREAT GOD AND KING

When we bow before our Great God and King
Lift our voices and praises sing
Thanking Him on His throne above
For showering on us His wondrous love

He informs us well on His will divine
Principals he encourages one and all obey
He forgives our sins and gives us strength
To stand firm in these final days
May we never take all this for granted
But earnestly do our utmost
To stand firm and lovingly serve our God
And sing praises with the Heavenly Host

Then when this system comes to an end
And we're all freed from Satan's hold
To receive life eternal in Paradise
God's word is worth more than gold

PARADISE RESTORED

May God above grant us to see
When wickedness on earth will no more be
And joy and peace and righteousness
On earth increase for all to see

Just to see Paradise restored
On earth Jehovah's love out poured
The Kingdom rule from heaven above
Under the rulership of His son of love

The name of Jehovah now glorified
His purposes for earth is magnified
No sickness sorrow death or pain
Ever to be on earth again

THE BRUNNER RANCH

I was born in Torrance County
Out in fair New Mexico
There were Rattlesnakes and Cactus
And Tumbleweeds that blow

Cattle grazed on Grama grass
We'd roundup in the Fall
Back then a man would tip his hat
And sing a friendly How-ya-all!

Range land lays off to the east
The Manzanos to the west
Pinto beans grown in between
O're the world known as the best

The dust storms of the Thirties
Drove many off the land
Through drought and depression many stayed
Determined to make a stand

We rode the range together
Two brothers side by side
Until that awful run away
When Grandad Brunner died

The Brunner ranch where I was born
Stands today in disrepair
It's now seen its glory days
Oh the history written there

If my life I could live over
One thing would surely change
I'd not live the city life
But choose the open range

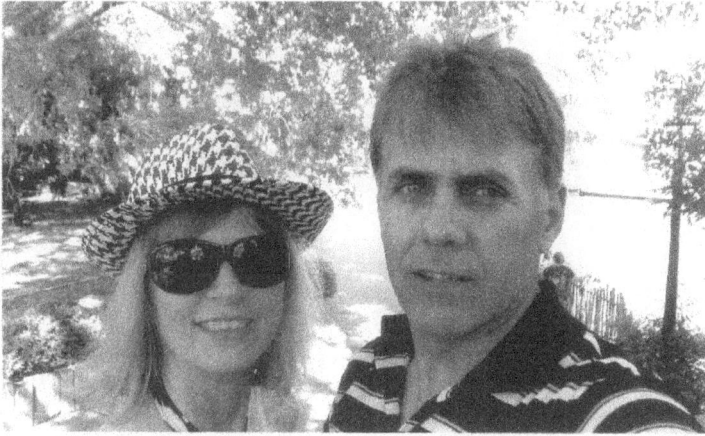

ACKNOWLEDGEMENT

Very special thanks to Clay Brazil for the outstanding illustrations. To his lovely wife June for her sacrificing time with her husband so he could ply his talent. I could never thank you enough Clay for your friendship and the dedication to capturing my "Reflections" in the poems. Truly, an exercise of the legacy handed to you by your father Joe. As well as a credit to your own natural ability and your Degree in Art from N.M.U. The schools of Estancia and Moriarty New Mexico are fortunate to have someone with such talent and integrity. I am a better man for having known you.

Your Friend
George Burns

ADDITIONAL CREDITS

Drovers; Karl and Debbie Larson for their
Computer expertise
Trail boss; daughter Shelley Cole
Without their contribution this herd would not
have come together and arrived at Trails End!

My never-ending gratitude as
Trail drivers
You are the Best!
Thanks George

Author: George C. Burns

www.ingramcontent.com/pod-product-compliance
Lightning Source LLC
LaVergne TN
LVHW092318080426
835509LV00034B/733